THE BOOK OF
GIVING

A TRIBUTE TO
MOTHER TERESA

WITH THE WORDS OF KAHLIL GIBRAN

———————•———————

Simon Weinstock

Anaya Publishers Ltd

LONDON

First published in Great Britain in 1990
by Anaya Publishers Ltd, 49 Neal Street, London WC2H 9PJ

Edited and produced by Grub Street, London

Designed by Stewart Austin

Copyright © 1990 Grub Street, London
Copyright photographs © 1990 Simon Weinstock

British Library Cataloguing in Publication Data
Weinstock, Simon
The Book of Giving: a tribute to Mother Teresa.
1. India (Republic). Catholic missions. Teresa, Mother, 1910–
I. Title
226.209

ISBN 1-85470-034-0

Typeset by Pearl Graphics, Hemel Hempstead
Originated by Hong Kong Reprohouse
Printed and bound in Italy by New Interlitho

The passage on giving from *The Prophet* by Kahlil Gibran is reproduced
here by kind permission of William Heinemann Ltd.

God bless you
Me Teresa mc

I first came across Kahlil Gibran's book *The Prophet* in the spring of 1988, when I listened to a tape of a well-known actor reading the passage on giving. I was quite moved by its simple message but it was not long before I had forgotten all about it. A short while later those same words were sent to me unprompted by a friend; 'How appropriate for today's world' I remember thinking, as I stuffed the book back into the envelope in which it had arrived, and unceremoniously placed it under a ton of other unloved never-quite-know-what-to-do-with-mail.

During the following weeks however, I noticed that some of the words had started to punctuate my otherwise mundane and restless thoughts. From the bottom of my mail mountain I retrieved with curiosity the volume and re-read the words. This time some deep and resonant chord resounded inside me and I was moved to tears. I probably wasn't the first to feel like that about these words, and I knew then that somehow they were going to be of great significance to my life for I had never been so moved by anything before. Suddenly I wanted everyone to read them and hopefully also be touched by them. How could I share their beautiful message with as many people as possible? What could just one individual do?

Finally, an idea came to me, to seek out the one person in the world who, to me, epitomized this spirit of giving, Mother Teresa. I would ask her permission to photograph the work she does and use the pictures to illustrate the words of Gibran for a book. I should point out that this seemed a pretty crazy idea at the time, partly because I am not a professional photographer, but mostly because I was petrified about the idea of leaving my comfortable life and heading for Calcutta.

I knew then that I must pursue the progress of the book with absolute honesty and integrity, and not for any personal gain, if its message was to succeed into today's cynical society – and this thought would fortify me many times in the often difficult months ahead.

Many people I met who knew Mother Teresa warned me that she would not allow such a project and I realized how easy it would be to give up immediately. But I chose not to. . . .

Riddled with fear and pessimism, I gave up everything I was doing and flew to Calcutta. Within this seething mass of humanity I found many others who likewise informed me of the doomed nature of this book. My fear of even asking Mother Teresa for permission had now grown out of all proportion. How many of us fear to ask for what we want because we are afraid of what the answer might be? How easily are we put off our goals, however small, by the fear of rejection?

Calcutta is a teeming city, overwhelmed by

problems. It is also a beautiful, majestic, albeit crumbling city, containing a wealth of extraordinary individuals whose sheer determination to survive often against the cruelest and most overwhelming of odds can leave the casual observer aghast. That this city is home to the woman known as 'The Living Saint' can come as no surprise to anyone fortunate enough to have spent some time there. It is a city I have come to know a little and love a lot.

Learning that Mother Teresa was out of the country, I resolved to do some voluntary work in her home for the Destitute and Dying at Kalighat in Calcutta. The thought of working among death and disease in such a place filled me with an abject terror so great, it was not until 5 days later that I summoned up enough courage to go. Prior to this, my life had been spent in television advertising and I had never knowingly been lauded for my social work! Carrying dead bodies to the local burning ghat every morning; washing, drying, shaving, toileting and spoon feeding the often outrageously deformed men was a very far cry indeed from standing around in a London film studio arguing with other grown men the appropriate merits of tea spoon handles for a Yoghurt commercial! The daily washing by hand of fifty or so soiled and disease-infested blankets could best be described as a true labour of love. The work was extraordinary, and so deeply moved was I by its nature that I ended up staying there for over a month – far longer than the day or two I had originally intended. The meaning of Gibran's words were beginning to come to life for me.

Hearing of the return of Mother Teresa from the Sudan, I presented myself at the end of a short line of people waiting to receive her blessing after Morning Mass at the Mother House where she lives. I was extremely nervous about meeting her but as I came to stand in front of this diminutive woman, her large leathered hands outstretched in a gesture of openness and blessing, my fear was melted by her warm, radiant smile and her most gentle demeanour. I felt at once both humbled and uplifted.

Explaining my mission, I handed her a copy of *The Prophet* and she suggested I return the following day. When I returned she said she didn't think she could give me permission. Could all these doom-mongers be right – was this the end of my undertaking? I remember thinking 'Well she hasn't said NO'. I stood there motionless, silently staring at her for what seemed like an hour – it was probably ten seconds. Then something happened; she suggested I return again in a few days time. Unseen spiritual forces seemed to be at work. Maybe the words of Gibran were taking on a life of their own. Returning twice more I was eventually handed a slip of paper which turned out to be a letter of introduction – it said simply 'Please allow Mr Simon Weinstock to take a few photographs of our work' and was signed by Mother Teresa herself. I was so thrilled I went to bed for the rest of the day.

The photographs in this book are the result of the rest of my four months stay in Calcutta working with and around the Sisters and Brothers of the Missionaries of Charity. They represent a personal interpretation of just a small part of their life's endeavour. My experiences there were life enhancing and I learnt at first hand the meaning of Gibran's words through Mother Teresa's work. I know I will return many more times.

In keeping with the spirit of this book, I had given some considerable thought to the question of royalties and decided I would like to give them all to Mother Teresa – it never occurred to me for one moment that there would be a problem with this.

At our last meeting in December 1989 she had been out of hospital only a few days having had a pacemaker fitted. She looked fit and well and as always my initial nervousness was somehow calmed as soon as she spoke. I asked if she would accept the royalties from the book and to my astonishment she replied quietly but firmly that no-one is to raise money in her name – she believes only in Divine Intervention, she repeated this a number of times. I understood that if I personally wished to give the money to her organisation then that would be fine.

She said 'Give until it hurts, Give until it hurts' like some wizened old carpenter chipping away at a lump of rotten wood with a gold chisel. 'Give until it hurts' – this is the message of Mother Teresa.

I am not a particularly religious person and so I still struggle enormously with the significance of my experience yet I somehow feel blessed that this book has come to fruition. I hope that it will be a simple yet fitting tribute to a woman whose spirit has transformed the lives of so many and that in some small way at least one more person may be similarly touched – you!

Simon Weinstock

KAHLIL GIBRAN

Kahlil Gibran was born on the 6th December 1883 in Bcharre, Lebanon, a town at the foot of the Cedar Mountain. His mother was a widow with one son when she married Gibran's father, a hearty impractical, extrovert whose addictions to coffee, cigarettes and alcohol were likewise years later to afflict Gibran in equal measure.

In 1894, when Gibran was eleven, his mother left her husband and taking him, his half brother and two younger sisters, emigrated to the USA, where they settled into the poor Chinatown area of Boston. During the next few years, Gibran shunned the childish activities of his contemporaries as he pursued his solitary passion for drawing and literature. By the age of fourteen his artistic talent had attracted the attention of a beautiful, wealthy but neglected businessman's wife. They became secret lovers until Gibran went to Beirut a year later to complete his Arabic education.

He left Lebanon forever in 1902 and returned to Boston. But within two years tragedy struck, depriving him of his beloved mother, two sisters and half brother, who all died of TB. Gibran was rescued from the depths of despair by a philanthropic headmistress Mary Haskell, who provided him with a monthly allowance for many years which enabled him to study in Paris at the Academy of Fine Arts. The profound grief and bitterness caused by the loss of his family was to become the fuel of his creative genius, spurring him to his unique articulations on the human spirit.

From 1912, Gibran spent the rest of his life in New York where he struggled to write and draw his inner world and achieve the recognition which was to come in 1923 with the publication of *The Prophet*. His writing shows the influence of Blake, and Nietzsche, whose doctrine of the godless, rebel superman particularly appealed to a Gibran tortured by his failure to live up to his ideals, yet driven to express them in his works of art.

He died in 1931 of cirrhosis of the liver and TB. Today *The Prophet* is a worldwide bestseller, translated into 20 languages.

MOTHER TERESA

The year, 1990, marks the 80th birthday of Mother Teresa. Sadly, because of poor health, it also marks the year of her retirement. For more than 60 years she has lived and worked in Calcutta devoting her life to 'whole-hearted and free service to the poorest of the poor', a vow she herself ordained. This she dispenses with the same indomitable spirit that can often be found in so many of those whom she serves. It is a daunting, never ending, and often thankless task that Mother Teresa administers with such joy and a love of selfless giving so immense it is little wonder that she has touched the hearts of so many. Her personal magnetism has attracted many thousands of people from all over the world, from beggars to kings, offering their help.

Born Agnes Gonxha Bojaxhiu on the 26th August 1910 in Skopje, Yugoslavia, it was at the age of twelve that she first discerned a vocation for working as a Missionary. At fifteen she was further inspired by stories reaching her from Calcutta about the work of the Lorretto nuns, and by the age of eighteen had been accepted as a postulant in their order at Rathfarnham in Dublin.

She arrived in Calcutta in 1929 and by 1931 had made her commitment to God by the Profession of the Three Vows. Assigned a teaching job, she was eventually to become headmistress of her school.

In 1946, on her way to the relative cool of Darjeeling for retreat, she received 'a call within a call'. So troubled had she become by the terrible sights, sounds and smells of the incumbent poverty she beheld, that she implored her superiors to allow her to leave the relative comfort of her convent and actually live amongst the poor, something normally never allowed. Permission was eventually granted and adopting as her form of dress a simple white cotton sari with a blue border, open-toed sandals and a small cross pinned to her shoulder, Sister Teresa began her new life in earnest.

Many people even today in Calcutta can be found lying in the streets dying, diseased, deformed, starving and naked and apart from starting a school for slum children, these were the people to whom Mother Teresa wanted to bring the love of God.

By 1954 she had opened a home for the Destitute and Dying within the precincts of a sacred Hindu temple called Kalighat. Initially as a religious outsider she was despised by the local people but when she was seen tending a dying Hindu priest whom no hospital would admit, their hearts soon turned.

She had by now been joined by a number of her former pupils and had inaugurated her own religious order The Missionaries of Charity.

The name, and the nature of her work spread rapidly, reaching a climax in 1979 when she was awarded the Nobel Prize for Peace. Even here she

asked that the gala dinner to be given in her name be cancelled and the money go instead to feeding the poor.

Often fighting shy of publicity, Mother Teresa frequently arrives unannounced in countries, sometimes where a natural disaster or political upheaval may have occurred, and other times to set up homes for the poor and needy whatever their requirements.

Today, she has over 420 homes in 90 countries around the world providing sustenance and love for many thousands of people; the dying and destitute, abandoned or homeless children and babies, the mentally ill, drug addicts, AIDS sufferers, alcoholics and lepers.... More than 3000 men and women of every nationality have joined her order, millions of others in many countries have formed an official organization called The Co-Workers of Mother Teresa and many, many more just turn up and help at one of the numerous homes. However, some of those arriving in Calcutta to help have been told to go back to their own countries and ensure that no-one there that they meet should ever feel lonely or rejected. This, Mother Teresa tells them in her own inimitable manner, is 'their Calcutta'.

Then said a rich man, Speak to us of Giving.

And he answered...

You give but little
when you give of your possessions.

It is when you give of yourself
that you truly give.

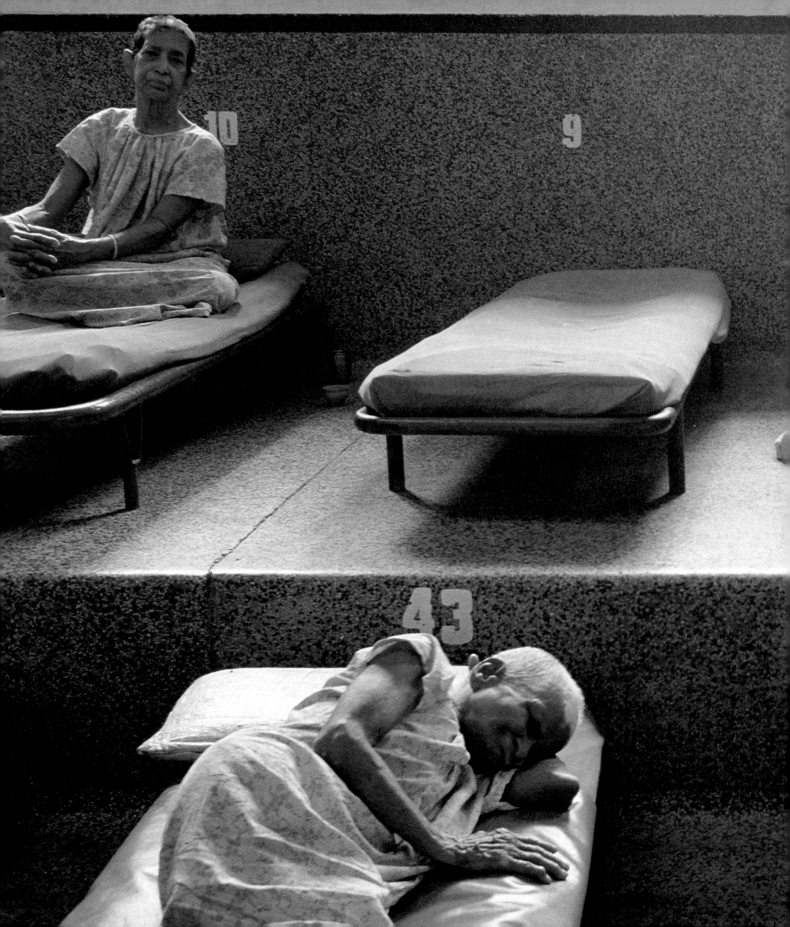

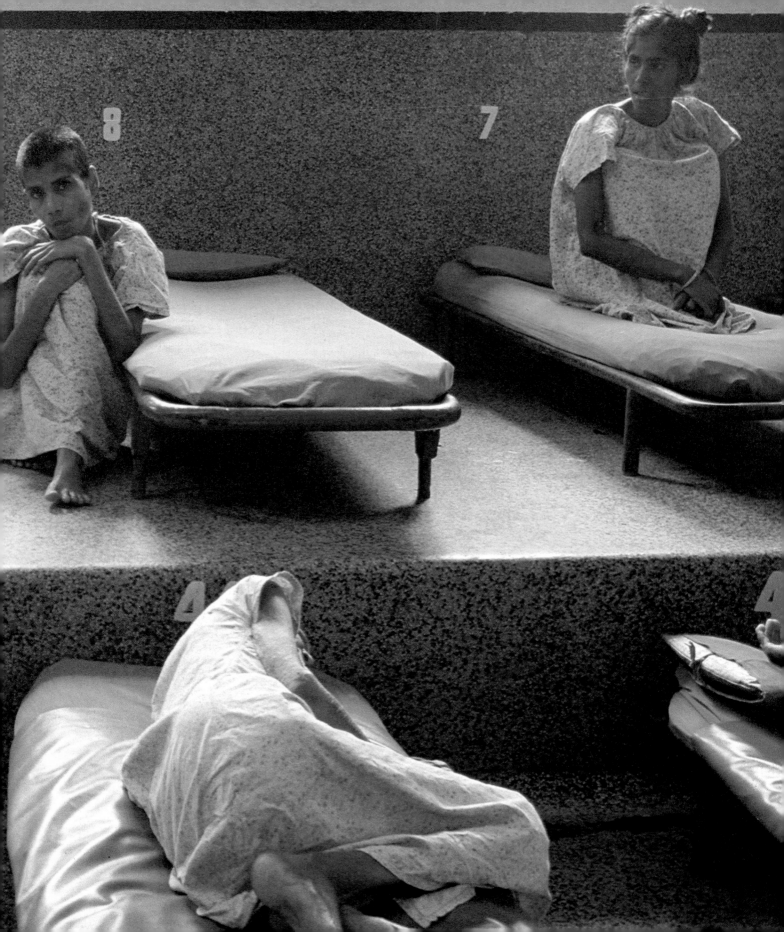

For what are your possessions
but things you keep and guard
for fear you may need them tomorrow?

And tomorrow, what shall tomorrow bring
to the over-prudent dog burying bones
in the trackless sand as he follows
the pilgrims to the holy city?

And what is fear of need but need itself?
Is not dread of thirst when your well is full,
the thirst that is unquenchable?

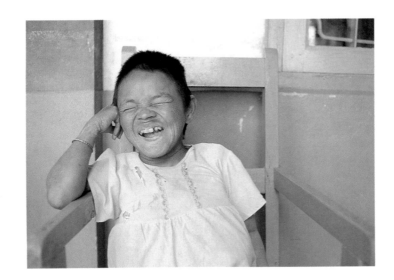

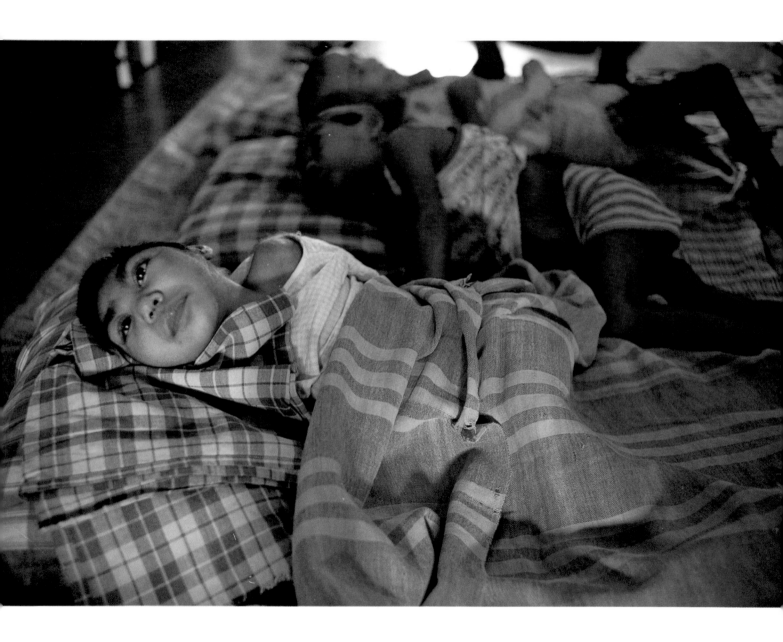

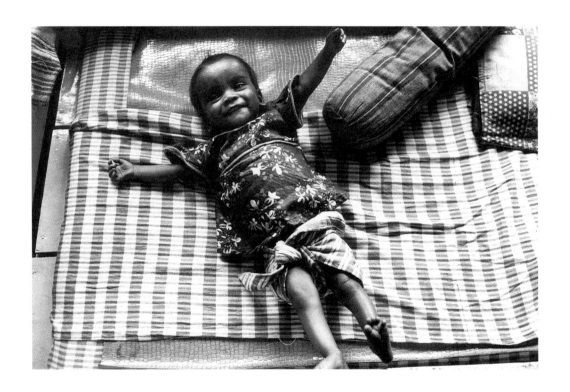

There are those who give little
of the much which they have –
and they give it for recognition
and their hidden desire
makes their gifts unwholesome.

And there are those who have little
and give it all.
These are the believers in life
and the bounty of life,
and their coffer is never empty.

There are those who give with joy,
and that joy is their reward.
And there are those who give with pain,
and that pain is their baptism.

And there are those who give
and know not pain in giving,
nor do they seek joy,
nor give with mindfulness of virtue;
They give as in yonder valley
the myrtle breathes its fragrance
into space.

Through the hands of such as these
God speaks, and from behind their eyes
He smiles upon the earth.

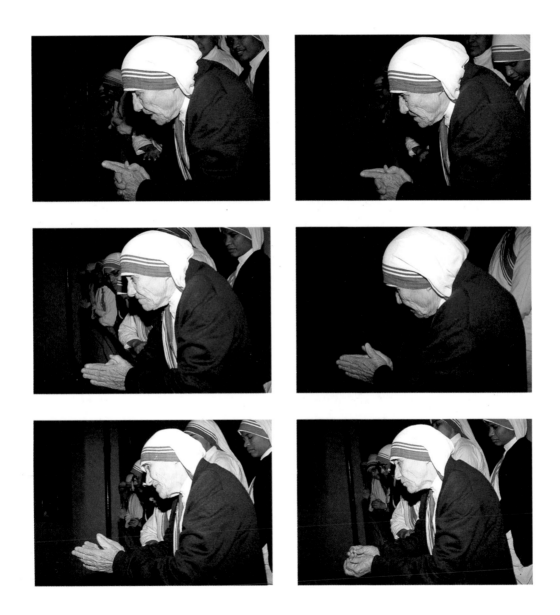

It is well to give when asked,
but it is better to give unasked,
through understanding;
And to the open-handed
the search for one who shall receive
is joy greater than giving.

And is there aught you would withhold?
All you have shall some day be given;
Therefore give now,
that the season of giving may be yours
and not your inheritors'.

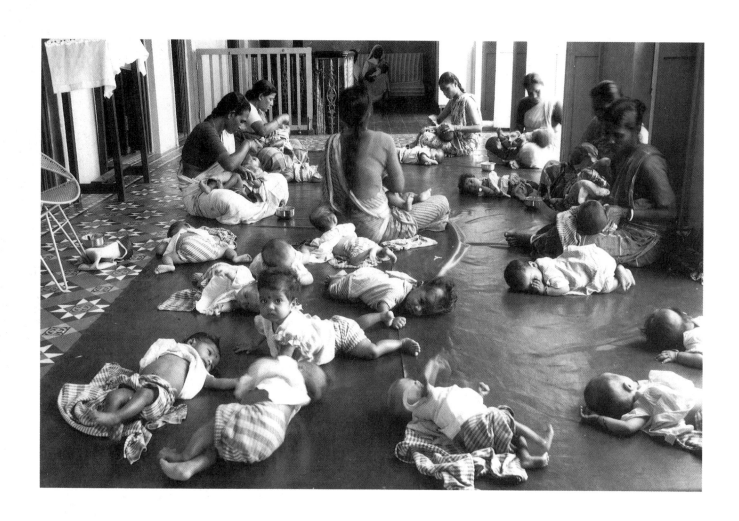

You often say, "I would give,
but only to the deserving."
The trees in your orchard say not so,
nor the flocks in your pasture.
They give that they may live,
for to withhold is to perish.

Surely he who is worthy
to receive his days and his nights
is worthy of all else from you.

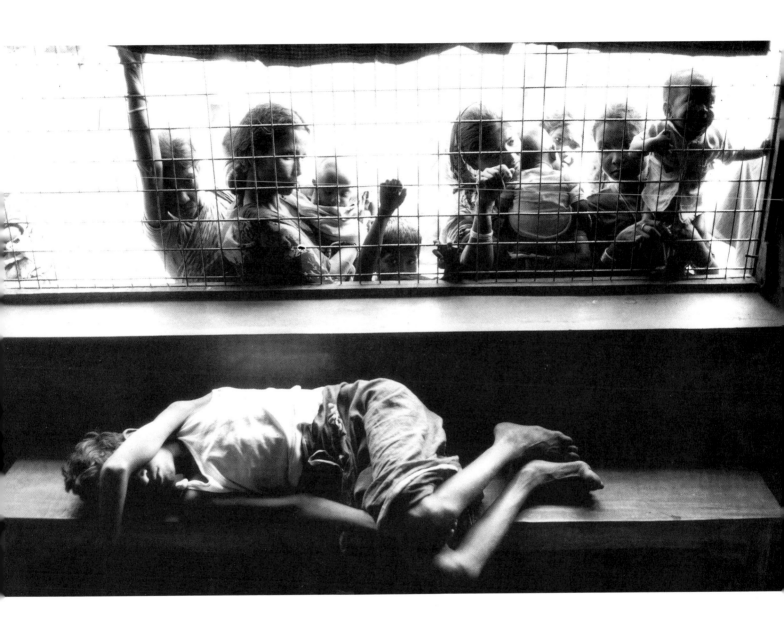

And he who has deserved
to drink from the ocean of life
deserves to fill his cup
from your little stream.

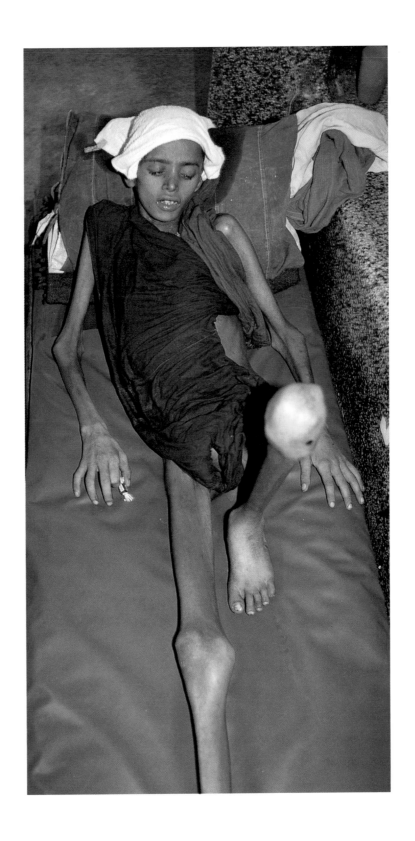

And what desert greater shall there be,
than that which lies in the courage
and the confidence, nay the charity,
of receiving?

And who are you that men
should rend their bosom
and unveil their pride,
that you may see their worth naked
and their pride unabashed?

See first that you yourself
deserve to be a giver,
and an instrument of giving.

For in truth
it is life that gives unto life —
while you, who deem yourself a giver,
are but a witness.

And you receivers —
and you are all receivers —
assume no weight of gratitude,
lest you lay a yoke upon yourself
and upon him who gives.

Rather rise together with the giver
on his gifts as on wings;
For to be overmindful of your debt
is to doubt his generosity
who has the free-hearted earth for mother,
and God for father.

PLATE LIST

This orphanage is situated in a relatively pleasant area of the city, hence its name.

32. A sister prepares to give an art lesson to slum children at Sealdah Railway Station, Calcutta.

33. Mother Teresa makes a point on giving after Midnight Mass, Christmas Eve, 1989. At Easter and Christmas especially, there are scenes of tremendous joy and excitement as she addresses everyone present after the service, from the balcony of the Mother House.

35. *Top*. A blind beggar woman squats on a street corner − very much a part of everyday life in Calcutta. It is said that up to three million people live this way. Though this may be an exaggeration, there is no doubt that the problem is immense.

35. *Bottom*. Seeking food and care on the streets, a young girl cradles her baby sister.

36. *Top*. Homelessness, Calcutta.
36. *Bottom*. The worldly possessions of a Calcutta street family: a parrot and an umbrella!

37. A never-ending and often thankless task − searching out the poor and needy on the streets of Calcutta. During the years of their training, the novices go out in the morning to the slums under the guidance of a professed sister.

38. Feeding time at Shishu Bhavan. There are various sections to the orphanage. One for the sick, another for normally healthy (and very boisterous) children, and a third for young and premature babies, where this photograph was taken. This is an area to which access is not normally allowed to vistors.

39. At the dispensary at Sealdah Station a woman begs help for her under-nourished grandson. She is just one amongst hundreds who turn up every morning and are given medical attention, food and milk powder for themselves and their children. Some mothers are so desperate for money they sell everything they are given, so the sisters insist on weighing the babies frequently and if they are found to be medically healthy but not gaining weight, no more food is given. This may seem harsh but is quite a common and fair way to deal with the rigorous realities of life in the Third World.

41. St. Mary's Church, Ripon Street, Calcutta, 1989. In the foreground are the novitiates taking final vows. As this is such an important event, all the local Catholic hierarchy are in attendance.

Off camera, the church is packed to bursting with the families of the novices, volunteers and other members of the order.

43. Women and children anxiously await the opening of the dispensary at Sealdah Station.

44. Novitiates gather in the courtyard of the Mother House prior to taking their final vows. A chalked notice on the blackboard tells its own story.

45. A busman's holiday: organized by an elderly Australian volunteer, known affectionately as 'Auntie Ella', postulants enjoy an extremely rare day off. Typically, they chose to spend it at Green Park, the orphanage near Calcutta airport.

47. Potty-training at Green Park.

48. A mother and young baby outside Kalighat waiting for food. Anything left over from feeding the residents is given to the poor outside.

49. A young boy is given love and care in his dying hours at Kalighat. The author carried his body to the burning ghat two days later.

51. Bath-time at Shishu Bhavan.

52. Mother Teresa at the inauguration of an extension to the Leprosarium, Titigarh, 1980.

53. A convocation of the Missionaries of Charity, 1980. Apparently, when Mother Teresa was asked who would succeed her when she died, she pointed to this photograph as her answer.

55. A perpetual reminder of Mother Teresa's philosophy at Shishu Bhavan, Lower Circular Road, Calcutta.

57. In the street outside the dispensary at Sealdah Station, a woman is resigned to waiting for food and medical attention for her baby.

59. A line of orphans wait patiently on their potties. Following this, the children are washed, dried and clothed every morning in a manner somewhat akin to a production line.

60-61. Mother Teresa in a typically humble and meditative pose, as she waits to present crosses to her newly professed sisters.

―――――――――――

All the photographs were taken by Simon Weinstock except those that appear on pages 20 (S Paul) and 52 and 53 (B Balen).

ACKNOWLEDGEMENTS

I would like to express my gratitude
and deep appreciation to the following people
for their invaluable support
during the creation of this book:

Carrie Rose, Virginia de Ledesma, Ann Candlish,
Stewart Austin, Henrietta Llewelyn Davies, Renee Mallardo,
Geoffrey Chiswick, Ann Blaikie, Kate Jones,
Carey Smith, Henrietta Rutherford Jones, Jane Lapotaire,
Phyllis and Father Manuel, Liz Wyse, Siobhan McGee,
'Auntie' Ella Williams, Sister Andrea,
and John Davies and Anne Dolamore at Grub Street
for believing it to be a possibility
and never questioning my sanity.

●

If you want to offer help or obtain any further information
about the work of the Missionaries of Charity please contact
Mrs Rosemary Noble, Fernhurst, West Road, St. George's
Hill, Weybridge, Surrey, England KT13 0LZ.